Richan's Miracle

Janet Robinson

BALBOA.
PRESS
A DIVISION OF HAY HOUSE

ISBN: 978-1-4525-4911-8 (sc)
ISBN: 978-1-4525-4910-1 (e)

Library of Congress Control Number: 2012906419

Balboa Press books may be ordered through booksellers or by contacting:

Balboa Press
A Division of Hay House
1663 Liberty Drive
Bloomington, IN 47403
www.balboapress.com
1-(877) 407-4847

Printed in the United States of America

Balboa Press rev. date: 04/06/12

For Richan, who survived three strokes
between 1999-2001. May the
Lord ever enfold you with His love.

Mom

Hi! My name is Richan, R-I-C-H-A-N, and I am 5 years old. I am in the hospital because I am very sick. There is something wrong with my brain. I had a stroke and even had a few seizures.

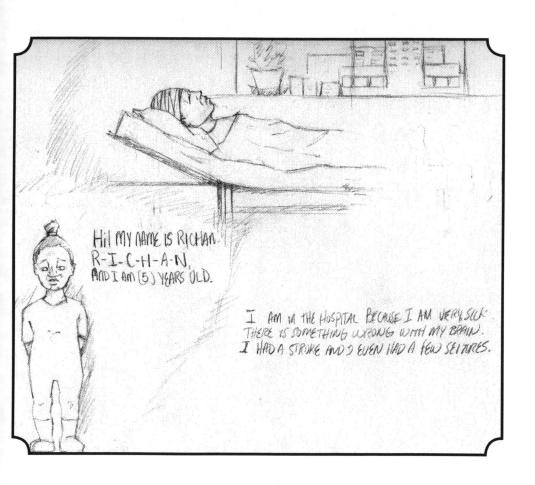

Hi! MY NAME IS RICHAN.
R-I-C-H-A-N,
AND I AM (5) YEARS OLD.

I AM IN THE HOSPITAL BECAUSE I AM VERY SICK.
THERE IS SOMETHING WRONG WITH MY BRAIN.
I HAD A STROKE AND I EVEN HAD A FEW SEIZURES.

When I couldn't move around I was very upset and I wanted to go home. I really hated being in the hospital.

However, when I started to get better I found out the most amazing thing: the hospital can be a grrreat place to be!

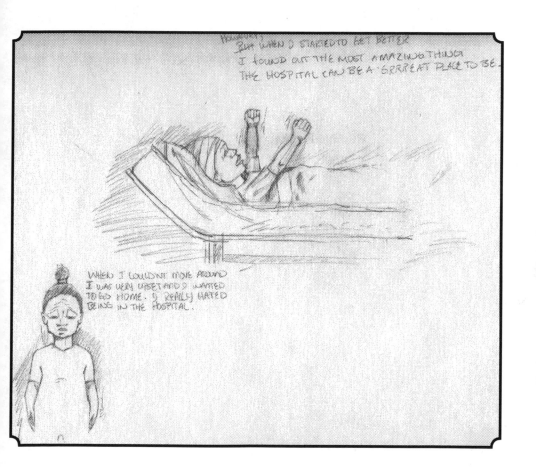

When I just got sick they used a stretcher to take me around. As I improved, I used a wheelchair.

WHEN I JUST GOT SICK THEY USED A
STRETCHER TO TAKE ME AROUND. AS I
IMPROVED I USED A WHEELCHAIR.

Now that I can walk again, I sometimes like to trick my mommy and ask for a wheelchair when we go for a walk because I really enjoy the ride. Even my cousin gets to push me around sometimes.

NOW THAT I CAN WALK AGAIN I SOMETIMES LIKE TO TRICK MY MOMMA AND ASK FOR A WHEELCHAIR WHEN WE GO FOR A WALK, BECAUSE I REALLY ENJOY THE RIDE, EVEN MY COUSIN GETS TO PUSH ME AROUND SOMETIMES.

I love to go to the playroom on my ward. We get to paint, colour, draw, read, play, watch television and do other fun things.

I like the volunteers. They help me to do and make all kinds of fun things. They also keep me company and read me lots of stories.

Sometimes I go to the Library when it is story time. We get to listen to the neatest stories which are read by some doctors. NEAT!

Then I get to choose and sign out all my favourite books like **Arthur**, **Franklin** and so many more.

I think I drive my Mom nuts because some days I borrow five books and she has to read them all to me.

I LIKE THE VOLUNTEERS. THEY
HELP ME TO DO AND MAKE ALL
KINDS OF FUN THINGS. THEY ALSO
KEEP ME COMPANY AND READ
ME LOTS OF STORIES.

SOMETIMES I GO TO
THE LIBRARY. WHEN IT'S
STORY TIME, WE GET TO
LISTEN TO THE NEATEST
STORIES WHICH ARE READ
BY SOME DOCTORS. NEAT!

THEN I GET TO CHOOSE AND
SIGN OUT ALL MY FAVOURITE
BOOKS — LIKE ARTHUR'S,
FRANKLIN, AND SO MANY MORE.
I THINK I DRIVE MY MOMMY
NUTS BECAUSE SOME DAYS
I BORROW 6 BOOKS AND SHE
HAS TO READ THEM ALL TO ME

I get to go to two different gyms everyday. My Mom says one is for phys---- something; it's a really long word. Mom says it's spelt: P-H-Y-S-I-O-T-H-E-R-A-P-Y. The other one is for something called O-C-C-U-P-A-T-I-O-N-A-L therapy.

I GET TO GO TO 2 DIFFERENT GYMS EVERY DAY.
MY MOM SAYS ONE IS FOR PHYS - - - SOMETHING,
IT'S A REALLY LONG WORD. MOM SAYS ITS SPELT:
P-H-Y-S-I-O- T-H-E-R-A-P-Y
THE OTHER ONE IS FOR SOMETHING CALLED OCCU-
PATI-O-N-A-L THERAPY.

I'm not sure what these words mean but, I do know I get to play the neatest games, bounce balls, climb, run and do all kinds of fun activities. I even play Hopscotch. I really like the gyms.

I'M NOT SURE WHAT THESE WORDS MEAN BUT I DO
KNOW I GET TO PLAY THE NEATEST GAMES, BOUNCE BALLS,
CLIMB, RUN, AND DO ALL KINDS OF FUN ACTIVITIES. I
EVEN PLAYED HOP SKOTCH. I REALLY LIKE THE GYMS.

One of my most favourite is the evening we go to the theatre and watch the funny play put on by some doctors, nurses, and volunteers. I like all the funny-looking characters and the songs. We even get a chance to win a prize. Wow!

One of my most favorite is the evening we go to the theater and watch the funnyday put on by some doctors, nurses and volunteers. I like all the funny-looking characters and the songs. We even get a chance to win a prize. Wow!

The best part of being in the hospital is that I get so many visitors. They all come to see how I am doing and they bring me lots of presents, treats and cards with money!

Oh, I still don't like medicines and I really hate I.V.'s, but, as I suffer.........

THE BEST PART OF BEING IN
IN THE HOSPITAL IS THAT I GET
SO MANY VISITORS. THEY ALL
COME TO SEE HOW I AM DOING
AND THEY BRING ME LOTS OF
PRESENTS, TREATS AND CARDS
WITH MONEY!

OH, I STILL DON'T LIKE
MEDICINES AND I REALLY HATE
I.V.'S, BUT AS I SUFFER...

...through those: I know that I'll be able to do something fun when they are done.

THROUGH THOSE, I KNOW THAT I'LL BE ABLE TO DO SOMETHING FUN WHEN THEY ARE DONE.

I can't believe it! The doctor just told my Mom that they are sending me home, TODAY!

Maybe I should pretend to get sick again!

MAYBE I SHOULD PRETEND TO WET SILK AGAIN!

Author's Postscript

It was the summer of 1999 when our daughter, Richan, had her first stroke. For me, at the time, it was inconceivable that a five year old could be paralyzed on one side, unable to speak, in a coma, ... We spent four weeks in hospital and months in rehab. She learned to walk, talk and to function independently again.

Then, in the spring of 2001 she had her second stroke. We went through it all again, and she recovered. What do you know? By the end of summer 2001, she had stroke number 3. Our family was devastated, but many people prayed, and miraculously, she recovered from the third stroke and is doing very well today.

I thank God for healing her. I thank all those who prayed for her. I thank all the medical personnel — hospital and rehab — who helped through her illnesses.

Janet Robinson, March 2012.

The author, Janet Robinson, is a certified Ontario teacher who enjoys writing in her spare time. She is married and lives with her family in Oshawa, Ontario.

http://www.richansmiracle.com

Mark Graham, the illustrator, lives and works in Whitby, Ontario. He works in all types of media.

Pictures

Richan just before she became ill

She's about 7 here

She's 6 years old and at a wedding with
her sisters, Shelly-Ann and Grace

She's graduating Grade
8 - June 2008

She's graduating High School - March 2012

Family picture at her Gr. 8 Grad June 2008

Additional family at Gr. 8 Grad, June 2008

Mark drew this family portrait from photographs in November of 2002

Printed in the United States
By Bookmasters

Morality and Freedom:

✦

America's Dynamic Duo

Reverend Steven Louis Craft, M. Div

iUniverse, Inc.
New York Bloomington

Morality and Freedom

America's Dynamic Duo

iUniverse books may be ordered through booksellers or by contacting:

iUniverse
1663 Liberty Drive
Bloomington, IN 47403
www.iuniverse.com
1-800-Authors (1-800-288-4677)

ISBN: 978-1-4401-0036-9 (pbk)
ISBN: 978-1-4401-0179-3 (ebk)

Printed in the United States of America

Contents

v

Introduction

A quote attributed to Alexis de Tocqueville...

"I sought for the greatness and genius of America in her commodious harbors and her ample rivers and it was not there; in her fertile fields and boundless forests and it was not there; in her rich mines and her vast commerce and it was not there; in her democratic Congress and her matchless Constitution and it was not there. Not until I went into the churches of America and heard her pulpits aflame with righteousness did I understand the secret of her genius and power. *America is great because America is good, and if America ever ceases to be good, she will cease to be great."*

It is my solemn conviction that the truth of those words has been clearly established!

Quoting the Rev. Charles Finney...

"The Church must take right ground in regard to politics...The time has come that Christians must vote for honest men and women and take consistent ground in politics...Christians have been exceedingly guilty in this matter. But the time has come when they must act differently...God cannot sustain this free and blessed country which we love and pray for unless the Church will take right ground...It seems sometimes as if the foundations of the nation are becoming rotten, and Christians seem to act as if they think God does not see what they do in politics. But I tell you He

does see it, and He will bless or curse this nation according to the course Christians take in politics."
The famous Nineteenth Century Evangelist further believed…

"If there is a decay of conscience, the pulpit is responsible for it. If the public press lacks moral discernment, the pulpit is responsible for it. If the church is degenerate and worldly, the pulpit is responsible for it. If the world loses its interest in Christianity, the pulpit is responsible for it. If our politics become so corrupt that the very foundations of our government are ready to fall away, the pulpit is responsible for it."

As a Minister of the Gospel, I write and speak on the subject…_Morality and Freedom: America's Dynamic Duo_ because of the increasing tendency of American politics to emphasize the importance of social programs at the expense of traditional moral standards. Secular Humanists in the political arena are seeking to repackage the same old sins of the past and convince the public they have "new solutions." They claim to have new political "wisdom", which is often nothing more than wickedness! _Pro-Abortion and Sexual Perversion_ are two prime examples of this folly!

Quoting Danny Hahlbohm…"Life is full of players, so it's really hard to know just who you truly can believe, and it's best to take it slow. For many have been led astray by men who have been deceived, as on their own they build their thrones on the things that they believe. God's ways are not our ways, but it is the Lord who rules, and they build the house as they see fit is the wisdom of a fool." (Ref. Isaiah 55:8–9) (Ref. Matthew 7:24–27)

A common aspect of immorality is the fact that in spite of the consequences attached to such behavior, the "voice of seduction" whispers and says, "This won't happen to you!" Due to changing mores, education, sophistication, technology, and a disdain for traditional morality, many now believe that departing from sound moral principles and ethical standards will be without consequences. (Ref. Galatians 6:7–8)

However, faithful adherence to Biblical principles, during the founding of America was so common it was considered to be the American way of life. It was the source of strength that enabled thirteen colonies to unite in the face of extreme danger and overwhelming odds, going on to defeat the most powerful nation on Earth at that time!

Americans won their independence, for the sake of establishing a nation where freedom, and liberty were to be defined as Inalienable Rights, given by God the Creator, whose precepts found in the Bible were regarded as the only sure foundation for Law and Government. As a result of this "Rock Solid Foundation," America went on to become the most powerful and prosperous nation on the face of the Earth! (Ref. Psalms 33:12)

Quoting Tocqueville…

"America is still the place where the Christian Religion has kept the greatest real power over men's souls; and nothing better demonstrates how useful and natural it is to man, since the country where it now has the widest sway is both the most enlightened and the freest."

I contend, as a Minister of the Gospel of Christ, that Christianity must be considered as the foundation on which the whole structure of America stands. Laws will have no permanent power without the sanction of Christian morality. This includes a firm belief that there is a Power above us that will reward our virtues and punish our vices. This we must rely on for the purity and permanence of freedom. That was the religion of the Founders of our Constitutional Republic, and they expected it to remain the religion of their descendants! (Ref. Psalms 11:3)

For over 150 years, Biblically-based morality and ethics served America well as a nation. There is an old saying, "If it ain't broke, don't fix it." Today, secular humanists have been undermining Christian values, and America has undergone a severe diminishing of traditional morality, stability, global image and reputation. When moral standards are sacrificed on the altar of secularism, the overall impact on society is increased spiritual deprivation. This dramatic degradation of American morality is the inevitable result of the fact that sincere recognition of God, who is the Source of all truth, sets the standard defining true morality and proper living, which has been cast aside in favor of so-called human wisdom. (Ref. John 8: 31–32) (Ref. John 14:6)

Nevertheless, secularists are still seeking to ignore the obvious, as they continue to convince the public that by increased human knowledge, science and technology, humanity will by means of social programs and political solutions, ignore sound moral principles without paying a devastating price for it! They would have us believe that in spite of the massive shifting of values that has taken place, we may still expect results which at one time basically everyone in America understood were dependent upon adherence to Biblical principles and the blessing of God Almighty! (Ref. Psalms 33:12) (Ref. Proverbs 14:34)

This is why secularists in the government today are relentlessly seeking to diminish the influence of the Christian clergy on the politics of this nation. They, the secularists, have even gone so far as to use the IRS through tax–exemption laws to silence the church from speaking out on moral issues of the day.

Humanists today promote the doctrine of the sufficiency of mankind to solve our problems without a need for Biblical restraints as guidelines for our conduct, or as a foundation for Law and Government. Humanists believe that by means of human intellect and reason alone, we are capable of forming programs that will solve problems, which were in themselves, created by many years in defiance of sound morals and principles based in Scripture. During this time period, we in America have been heading down a path of moral self-destruction, as evidenced by problems initiated and compounded by an explosion of filth and immorality. Abortion, homosexuality, pornography, violence, murder, theft, etc., etc., etc., have become mainstream, while traditional morality has been forced into the "closet!" The gradual and systematic removal of Christian morality and influence in this nation are at the root of many of our problems.

Secularists are convinced that liberal political philosophy, void of any religious principle, will bring forth a utopia, where misery and vice will be vanquished and the human race will reach a state of perfection. Regardless of how it is repackaged, it is still the age-old lie employed by the serpent in the Garden of Eden… namely "*You will be as God, knowing Good and Evil*"(Genesis 3:4–5) (Ref. Jeremiah 2:13). It wasn't true then, and it isn't true now!

In the following chapters of *Morality and Freedom: America's Dynamic Duo*, we will discuss how "*We Had It*" (Chapter One), how "*We Lost It*"—that foundation (Chapter Two), and how "*It's Time to Get It Back*"(Chapter Three).

Stay tuned, and may God continue to speak to your heart!

Chapter One

"We Had It"

July Fourth, Independence Day, reminds us that America separated from Britain, not God and His Commandments!

The Declaration of Independence began with these words:

"When in the Course of human Events it becomes necessary for one People to dissolve the Political Bands which have connected them with another, and to assume among the Powers of the Earth, the separate and equal Station to which the Laws of Nature and of Nature's God entitle them, a decent Respect to the Opinions of Mankind requires that they should declare the causes which impel them to the Separation."

"We hold these Truths to be self-evident, that all Men are created equal, that they are endowed by their Creator with certain unalienable Rights, that among these are Life, Liberty, and the Pursuit of Happiness. That to secure these Rights, Governments are instituted among Men, deriving their just Powers from the Consent of the Governed. That whenever any Form of Government becomes destructive of these Ends, it is the Right of the People to alter or to abolish it, and to institute new Government, laying its

Foundation on such Principles, and organizing its Powers in such Forms, as to them shall seem most likely to effect their Safety and Happiness."

The Declaration of Independence ended with these words: "We, Therefore the Representatives of the United States of America, In General Congress, Assembled, appealing to the Supreme Judge of the world for the rectitude of our intentions, do, in the Name, and by the authority of the good People of these Colonies, solemnly Publish and Declare, That These United Colonies are, and of Right ought to be, Free And Independent States; that they are Absolved from all Allegiance to the British Crown, and that all political connection between them and the State of Great Britain, is and ought to be totally dissolved; and that as Free and Independent States, they have full Power to levy War, conclude Peace, contract Alliances, establish Commerce, and to do all other Acts and Things which Independent States, may of right do. And for the support of this Declaration, with a firm reliance on the protection of Divine providence, We mutually pledge to each other our Lives, our Fortunes, and our sacred Honor."

Secular Humanists want you to believe otherwise, but the truth of the matter is the fact that the Declaration of Independence separated the Thirteen Colonies from Britain, not God! The Declaration further establishes that the Founders put their faith in God, and did not intend a separation from God! In fact the Constitution ends with these solemn words: "Done in convention by the unanimous consent of the States present, the seventeenth of September in the year of our Lord one thousand seven hundred and eighty seven and of the independence of the United States of America the twelfth. In witness whereof we have hereunto subscribed our Names." George Washington, President and Deputy from Virginia. The term "Our Lord" obviously referred to Jesus Christ!

The First Amendment was intended to prevent the establishment of a national church and to protect the free exercise of religion. It was not intended to mandate governmental neutrality between religion and irreligion, and make agnosticism or secularism the national religion!

Neither the Founders nor the States expected or desired the United States Supreme Court to try to erect a "wall of separation" between God and the Government. We shall now list the original Preambles of each State to establish this fact.

Alabama Preamble 1901, *"We, the people of the State of Alabama, invoking the favor and guidance of Almighty God, do ordain and establish the following Constitution."*

<u>Alaska Preamble 1956</u>, *"We, the people of Alaska, grateful to God and to those who founded our nation and pioneered this great land..."*

<u>Arizona Preamble 1911</u>, *"We, the people of the State of Arizona, grateful to Almighty God for our liberties, do ordain this Constitution."*

<u>Arkansas Preamble 1874</u>, *"We, the people of the State of Arkansas, grateful to Almighty God for the privilege of choosing our own form of government..."*

<u>California Preamble 1879</u>, *"We, the People of the State of California, grateful to Almighty God for our freedom..."*

<u>Colorado Preamble 1876</u>, *"We, the people of Colorado, with profound reverence for the Supreme Ruler of Universe..."*

<u>Connecticut Preamble 1818</u>, *"The People of Connecticut, acknowledging with gratitude the good Providence of God in permitting them to enjoy..."*

<u>Delaware Preamble 1897</u>, *"Through Divine Goodness all men have, by nature, the rights of worshipping and serving their Creator according to the dictates of their consciences."*

<u>Florida Preamble 1885</u>, *"We, the people of the State of Florida, grateful to Almighty God for our constitutional liberty, establish this Constitution."*

<u>Georgia Preamble 1777</u>, *"We, the people of Georgia, relying upon protection and guidance of Almighty God, do ordain and establish this Constitution."*

<u>Hawaii Preamble 1959</u>, *"We, the people of Hawaii, Grateful for Divine Guidance, Establish this Constitution."*

<u>Idaho Preamble 1889</u>, *"We, the people of the State of Idaho, grateful to Almighty God for our freedom, to secure its blessings..."*

<u>Illinois Preamble 1870</u>, *"We, the people of the State of Illinois, grateful to Almighty God for the civil, political and religious liberty which*

He hath so long permitted us to enjoy and looking to Him for a blessing on our endeavors."

Indiana Preamble 1851, *"We, the People of the State of Indiana, grateful to Almighty God for the free exercise of the right to choose our form of government."*

Iowa Preamble 1857, *"We, the People of the State of Iowa, grateful to the Supreme Being for the blessings hitherto enjoyed, and feeling our dependence on Him for a continuation of these blessings, establish this Constitution."*

Kansas Preamble 1859, *"We, the people of Kansas, grateful to Almighty God for our civil and religious privileges establish this Constitution..."*

Kentucky Preamble 1891, *"We, the people of the Commonwealth, are grateful to Almighty God for the civil, political and religious liberties."*

Louisiana Preamble 1921, *"We, the people of the State of Louisiana, grateful to Almighty God for the civil, political and religious liberties we enjoy."*

Maine Preamble 1820, *"We, the People of Maine, acknowledging with grateful hearts the goodness of the Sovereign Ruler of the Universe in affording us an opportunity and imploring His aid and direction."*

Maryland Preamble 1776, *"We, the people of the State of Maryland, grateful to Almighty God for our civil and religious liberty..."*

Massachusetts Preamble 1780, *"We, the people of Massachusetts, acknowledge with grateful hearts, the goodness of the Great Legislator of the Universe in the course of His Providence, an opportunity and devoutly imploring His direction."*

Michigan Preamble 1908, *"We, the people of the State of Michigan, grateful to Almighty God for the blessings of freedom establish this Constitution."*

Minnesota Preamble 1857, *"We, the people of the State of Minnesota, grateful to God for our civil and religious liberty, and desiring to perpetuate its blessings..."*

Mississippi Preamble 1890, *"We, the people of Mississippi, in convention assembled, grateful to Almighty God, and invoking His blessing on our work..."*

Missouri Preamble 1845, *"We, the people of Missouri, with profound reverence for the Supreme Ruler of the Universe, and grateful for His goodness...Establish this Constitution..."*

Montana Preamble 1889, *"We, the people of Montana, grateful to Almighty God for the blessings of liberty establish this Constitution."*

Nebraska Preamble 1875, *"We, the people, grateful to Almighty God for our freedom, establish this Constitution."*

Nevada Preamble 1864, *"We, the people of the State of Nevada, grateful to Almighty God for our freedom, establish this Constitution."*

New Hampshire Preamble 1792, *"Every individual has a natural and unalienable right to worship God according to the dictates of his own conscience."*

New Jersey Preamble 1844, *"We, the people of the State of New Jersey, grateful to Almighty God for civil and religious liberty which He hath so long permitted us to enjoy, and looking to Him for a blessing on our endeavors."*

New Mexico Preamble 1911, *"We, the People of New Mexico, grateful to Almighty God for the blessings of liberty..."*

New York Preamble 1846, *"We, the people of the State of New York, grateful to Almighty God for our freedom, in order to secure its blessings..."*

North Carolina Preamble 1868, *"We, the people of the State of North Carolina, grateful to Almighty God, the Sovereign Ruler of Nations, for our civil, political, and religious liberties, and acknowledging our dependence upon Him for the continuance of those."*

North Dakota Preamble 1889, *"We, the people of North Dakota, grateful to Almighty God for the blessings of civil and religious liberty, do ordain."*

Ohio Preamble 1852, *"We, the people of the state of Ohio, grateful to Almighty God for our freedom, to secure its blessings and to promote our common..."*

Oklahoma Preamble 1907, *"Invoking the guidance of Almighty God, in order to secure and perpetuate the blessings of liberty, establish this..."*

Oregon Preamble 1857, *"All men shall be secure in the Natural right, to worship Almighty God according to the dictates of their consciences."*

Pennsylvania Preamble 1776, *"We, the people of Pennsylvania, grateful to Almighty God for the blessings of civil and religious liberty, and humbly invoking His guidance..."*

Rhode Island Preamble 1842, *"We, the People of the State of Rhode Island, grateful to Almighty God for the civil and religious liberty which He hath so long permitted us to enjoy, and looking to Him for a blessing."*

South Carolina Preamble 1778, *"We, the people of the State of South Carolina, grateful to God for our liberties, do ordain and establish this Constitution."*

South Dakota Preamble 1889, *"We, the people of South Dakota, grateful to Almighty God for our civil and religious liberty..."*

Tennessee Preamble 1796, *"That all men have a natural and indefeasible right to worship Almighty God according to the dictates of their conscience."*

Texas Preamble 1845, *"We, the People of the Republic of Texas, acknowledging, with gratitude, the grace and beneficence of God."*

Utah Preamble 1896, *"Grateful to Almighty God for life and liberty, we establish this Constitution."*

Vermont Preamble 1777, *"Whereas all government ought to enable the individuals who compose it to enjoy their natural rights, and other blessings which the Author of Existence has bestowed on man."*

Virginia Preamble 1776, *"Religion, or the Duty which we owe our Creator can be directed only by Reason and it is the mutual duty of all to practice Christian Forbearance, Love and Charity towards each other."*

Washington Preamble 1889, *"We, the People of the State of Washington, grateful to the Supreme Ruler of the Universe for our liberties, do ordain this Constitution."*

West Virginia Preamble 1872, *"Since through Divine Providence we enjoy the blessings of civil, political and religious liberty, we, the people of West Virginia reaffirm our faith in and constant reliance upon God."*

Wisconsin Preamble 1848, *"We, the people of Wisconsin, grateful to Almighty God for our freedom..."*

Wyoming Preamble 1890, *"We, the people of the State of Wyoming, grateful to God for our civil, political, and religious liberties, establish this Constitution."*

Question:

Where is this so-called "Wall of Separation" between God and Country? When I was a child, we sang:

"Oh beautiful, for spacious skies, for amber waves of grain, for purple mountains majesties above the fruited plain! America! America! God shed His grace on thee. And crown thy good with brotherhood, from sea to shining sea.

Oh beautiful for pilgrim feet, whose stern, impassioned stress a thoroughfare for freedom beat across the wilderness! America! America! God mend thine every flaw. Confirm thy soul in self-control, thy liberty in law!"

When I was a child, we had been taught about the proud history and heritage of America. We weren't taught out of revisionist textbooks, which have replaced our Judeo-Christian heritage. We were taught about the influence of Biblical principles on the formation of law and government, and the role God played in the birth and establishment of America!

Despite America's miraculous beginning, and the unparalleled success that followed, America has forgotten God and has been lying down with the enemy of secular humanism. In America, today, we stand in grave danger of waking up during a time of severe crisis and finding that God has lifted His protective hand from us! I believe 9/11 was only the beginning of sorrows! There are many ways for a nation to be conquered from without and within! Immorality is one of them! If we fail to return to God soon, America will be conquered without a shot being fired, and we will lose our national sovereignty and subsequent freedom! The groundwork is already being laid for a globalist takeover through those who want to remove God from our foundations! (Ref. Psalms 9:17) (Ref. Proverbs 29:2)

Until recently, Americans benefited from being part of a truly God-ordained nation, that is, a nation chosen and set apart by God that prospers, but also abides under the shadow of His protection. Due to a profound Biblical influence on this nation, Americans have enjoyed an unprecedented level of blessings and success that has come as a result of Divine favor. These blessings have enabled America to accomplish God's purposes throughout the world. (Ref. Psalms 91:1–2)

America went through a phenomenal rise in global stature, and the blessings of God were evident in our schools, universities, businesses, and political institutions. When you consider the challenges, obstacles, and the odds against us, this was truly a miracle! God brought His people from all over the world to establish them together in America. Because of this, America became the "Land of the Free, and the Home of the Brave"! It was a sanctuary for those who had been persecuted, and a place of compassion and healing for the downtrodden. Unfortunately, we in America have been watching that blessing fade away! (Ref. Deuteronomy 28:7–8)

However, these blessings cannot be sustained, when the Christian Church remains silent in the face of rampant immorality and wickedness! This very thing is at the root of our most serious problems involving our lack of sound morality. Shameful things have now become "mainstream" such as abortion and homosexuality, and we are paying dearly for it! Despite the unprecedented immorality that is now pervasive in America, God has not taken His protective hand off of us completely. If He had, we would have already perished. But God has been allowing a progressive increase in the incidence and seriousness of problems that are plaguing our beloved nation. He is seeking to warn us that rebellion and immorality will completely destroy us. Natural disasters, terrorism, economic instability, deterioration of American education, deterioration of American industry, crime and violence, sexual promiscuity and perversion, and physical and mental illness are rampant.

These problems and more have been allowed by God to warn us of impending doom! God is pleading with us as a nation to turn back to Him in humility and repentance! I believe God has been preventing the total downfall of America for the sake of those true believers who truly love and serve Him!

Question for the Secular Humanists:

If all of our problems could be solved by human ability alone, why is it that the more advanced our science and technology becomes, the deeper we find ourselves buried under the filth of immorality and evil?

This situation will not change unless we have a spiritual awakening and a revival of traditional morality! There have been times throughout our history when America began to drift away from its Biblical foundations. When that happened, God dealt with it first by seeking to draw us back to Him with His tender mercies. When that failed, God then began to chasten and discipline us through crisis situations, such as terrorist attacks etc. For example, the First and Second Great Awakening in America prevented severe national immorality during the Eighteenth and Nineteenth Century.

Before the 1960's, most Americans still believed the birth of this nation was a work of God. Americans, by and large, were persuaded that our nation was born to be a "City Set on a Hill" and a "Light to the World!" As a result of such traditional beliefs, Americans were convinced that regardless of how difficult times became, God would always see us through and cause us to prosper! Thus, in times of national danger and distress, one of the first things to happen has been an emphasis on returning God to His rightful place in our nation. This has led many Americans to renew their commitment to God, both individually and corporately. When we as the American people join together in sincere prayer, seeking wisdom, comfort, and guidance from God, we draw spiritual strength to deal with difficult situations. (Ref. 2 Chronicles 7:14)

This type of spiritual response to national crisis is an American tradition that goes back to a time before the Revolutionary War. Faith in God and a conscience based on that faith, were the motivating factors in the hearts of many Americans during such times. This flowed out of a sense of reverence for God in the hearts of the people.

Today, however, there are fewer Americans who have the same unifying convictions out of which their decisions and actions flow. As a result, Americans are fighting among themselves with increasing intensity. When the Lord God is leading the people, there is unity, purpose, and strength among the people. But when reliance on God and submission to His will is lost, the result is chaos. Selfishness begins to rule, where true humility once reigned.

Fortunately, we are beginning to see a few American leaders rise up and call for a return to the principles of Biblical wisdom and traditional morality. We must stand with them or lose the liberty and freedom which once made us proud to be Americans!

As a Christian Minister of the Gospel, and a speaker on the issue of Morality for the John Birch Society, I would like to quote some of the Founders of America on this subject.

<u>John Adams</u>

"We have no government armed with power capable of contending with human passions unbridled by morality and religion. Avarice, ambition, revenge, or gallantry, would break the strongest cords of our Constitution as a whale goes through a net. Our Constitution was made only for a moral and religious people. It is wholly inadequate to the government of any other."

<u>Abigail Adams</u>

"A patriot without religion in my estimation is as great a paradox as an honest Man without the fear of God. Is it possible that he whom no moral obligations bind, can have any real Good Will towards Men? Can he be a patriot who, by an openly vicious conduct, is undermining the very bonds of Society? ...The Scriptures tell us "Righteousness exalteth a Nation."(Proverbs 14:34)

<u>John Adams</u>

"Statesmen, my dear Sir, may plan and speculate for liberty, but it is Religion and Morality alone, which can establish the Principles upon which Freedom can securely stand. "The only foundation of a free

Constitution is pure Virtue, and if this cannot be inspired into our People in a greater Measure, than they have it now, they may change their Rulers and the forms of Government, but they will not obtain a lasting liberty."

Sir William Blackstone

"Man, considered as a creature, must necessarily be subject to the laws of his Creator, for he is entirely a dependent being...And, consequently, as man depends absolutely upon his Maker for everything, it is necessary that he should in all points conform to his Maker's will...this will of his Maker is called the law of nature. These laws laid down by God are the eternal immutable laws of good and evil...This law of nature dictated by God Himself, is of course superior in obligation to any other. It is binding over all the globe, in all countries, and at all times: no human laws are of any validity if contrary to this..."

Patrick Henry

"It cannot be emphasized too strongly or too often that this great nation was founded not by religionists, but by Christians; not on religions, but on the Gospel of Jesus Christ. For this very reason peoples of other faiths have been afforded asylum, prosperity, and freedom of worship here."

"Bad men cannot make good citizens. A vitiated state of morals, a corrupted public conscience are incompatible with freedom."

John Jay

"Providence has given to our people the choice of their rulers, and it is the duty, as well as the privilege and interest of our Christian nation to select and prefer Christians for their rulers."

Thomas Jefferson

"He who permits himself to tell a lie once, finds it much easier to do it a second and third time, till at length it becomes habitual; he tells lies without attending to it, and truths without the world's believing him. This falsehood of the tongue leads to that of the heart, and in time depraves all its good dispositions."

"I never...believed there was one code of morality for a public and another for a private man."

James Madison

"We have staked the whole future of American civilization, not upon the power of government, far from it. We have staked the future of all of our political institutions upon the capacity of each and all of us to govern ourselves, to control ourselves, to sustain ourselves according to the Ten Commandments of God."

Benjamin Rush

"By removing the Bible from schools we would be wasting so much time and money in punishing criminals and so little pains to prevent crime. Take the Bible out of our schools and there would be an explosion in crime."

George Washington

"I hope that the foundation of our national policy will be laid in the pure and immutable principles of private morality. The preeminence of free government exemplifies by all the attributes which can win the affections of its citizens and command the respect of the world."

"Of all the dispositions and habits which lead to political prosperity, Religion and Morality are indispensable supports. In vain would that man claim the tribute of Patriotism, who should labor to subvert these great Pillars of human happiness, these firmest props of the duties of Men and Citizens."

Daniel Webster

"There is no nation on earth powerful enough to accomplish our overthrow. Our destruction, should it come at all, will be from another quarter. From the inattention of the people to the concerns of their government, from their carelessness and negligence. I must confess that I do apprehend some danger. I fear that they may place too implicit a confidence in their public servants and fail properly to scrutinize their conduct; that in this way they may be made the dupes of designing men and become the instruments of their own undoing."

"If religious books are not widely circulated among the masses in this country, I do not know what is going to become of us as a nation. If truth be not diffused, error will be; If God and His Word are not known and received, the devil and his works will gain the ascendancy, If the evangelical volume does not reach every hamlet, the pages of a corrupt and licentious literature will; If the power of the Gospel is not felt throughout the length and breadth of the land, anarchy and misrule, degradation and misery, corruption and darkness will reign without mitigation or end."

<u>Noah Webster</u>

"In my view, the Christian religion is the most important and one of the first things in which all children, under a free government ought to be instructed…No truth is more evident to my mind than that the Christian religion must be the basis of any government intended to secure the rights and privileges of a free people."

"The moral principles and precepts contained in the Scriptures ought to form the basis of all of our civil constitutions and laws…All the miseries and evils which men suffer from vice, crime, ambition, injustice, oppression, slavery and war, proceed from their despising or neglecting the precepts contained in the Bible."

"When you become entitled to exercise the right of voting for public officers, let it be impressed on your mind that God commands you to choose for rulers just men who will rule in the fear of God. The preservation of a republican government depends on the faithful discharge of this duty."(Ref. Proverbs 29:2a)

"If the citizens neglect their duty and place unprincipled men in office, the government will soon be corrupted; laws will be made not for the public good so much as for the selfish or local purposes.

"Corrupt or incompetent men will be appointed to execute the laws; the public revenues will be squandered on unworthy men; and the rights of the citizens will be violated or disregarded."

"If a republican government fails to secure public prosperity and happiness, it must be because the citizens neglect the divine commands, and elect bad men to make and administer the laws." (Ref. Proverbs 29:2b)

Some Personal Thoughts:

After reading these many quotes and preambles, it is my firm conviction that the greatest threat to our free republic is moral decline. It is politically correct today to ignore the relationship between morality and freedom. Liberty, they say, flourishes independently from moral standards, as long as we allow people to pursue their own lifestyle choices.

This lie is going to be the death of our beloved America, unless we wake up to the truth, that indeed, morality does matter!

The U. S. Constitution itself cannot stand successfully against the deterioration of sound moral principles. That is a problem no legal document can solve. It is also a fact that the government is usually a reflection of the people! We inherit the government we deserve. Since the 1960's large numbers of Americans have embraced immoral lifestyles that were once unthinkable! Same-sex "marriage" is just one case in point! This and many other spiritual, social, political and economic problems threaten to overwhelm us as a nation because of our own lack of moral restraint.

We must understand how important morality is to the survival of our constitutional republic. Those who object to laws that restrict vice do not see that people who are consumed with vice, whether alcohol, drugs, sexual perversion, gambling, prostitution, pornography, etc., are the enemies of true freedom, whether they realize it or not. Vice and immorality do not confine themselves to the person alone, but spread like a cancer throughout the society. Because private immorality also encourages public criminality, it also creates a demand for more government control such as increased law enforcement! This leads to a possible police state! Paradoxical as it may seem to some, legally discouraging vice and immorality actually enhances freedom, rather than suppressing it! We must put "moral chains" on our own sinful passions and appetites! Our passions must not be allowed to forge our fetters!

The primary responsibility for maintaining our moral standards abides not in the public sphere of government, but in our homes, churches, civic organizations, and in our own hearts!

Our motto in the John Birch Society is: "Less government, more responsibility, and with God's help a better world." The most important words in that motto are "with God's help." We can succeed in saving our great nation with the sustaining help of God and His grace. He will give us the strength to persevere, and He will change the hearts and minds of the American people to hunger and thirst after righteousness once again! Let it be, Dear Lord, Let it be!

Our Founding Fathers, for the most part, believed in "old school" or traditional morality, which is based upon spiritual and moral absolutes found in the Ten Commandments. The acts of each individual person, according to this system, are judged as either good or evil, moral or immoral, right or wrong. God Himself is the final Judge, basing His verdict on the Moral Law, namely the Ten Commandments. Traditional morality declares that idolatry, blasphemy, disobedience, irreverence, hatred, murder, adultery, theft, dishonesty, etc., etc., are wrong and are to be avoided by law-abiding citizens.

However, post-modern, secular humanists believe in "new morality," which is rooted in moral relativism and situational ethics. It believes and declares that moral absolutes do not exist and that each unique situation calls for an individual moral determination to discern good and evil, moral or immoral, right or wrong. To lie, cheat, steal, or murder, may or may not be immoral depending on the exact context of the situation at hand. This philosophy says the "end may justify the means."

For most of our nation's history, we in America, held fast to the notion of Biblical Traditional Morality, rooted in the Ten Commandments of God. Today, however, this is no longer the standard!

President George Washington believed that a high national morality could only be successfully maintained by strong religious principles. In his Farewell Address he declared:

"Of all the dispositions and habits which lead to political prosperity, Religion and Morality are indispensable supports. In vain would that man claim the tribute of patriotism, who should labor to subvert these great pillars of human happiness, these firmest props of the duties of men and citizens. The mere politician, equally with the pious man, ought to respect and cherish them. A volume could not trace all their connections with private and public felicity. Let it simply be asked, where is the security for prosperity, for reputation, for life, if the sense of religious obligation desert the oaths which are the instrument of investigation in courts of justice? And let us with caution indulge the supposition that morality can be maintained without religion. Whatever may be conceded to the influence of refined education on minds of peculiar structure, reason and experience both forbid us to expect that national morality can prevail in exclusion of religious principle."

America, we are the "Land of the Free, and the Home of the Brave." Our fundamental rights are given to us by our Creator God and not by government! We pledge allegiance to the flag of a nation "under God" indivisible, with Liberty and Justice for all! We are responsible if we neglect the deliberate undermining of our moral principles. We are responsible if we allow religion and morality to be banished from our government and schools. We are responsible if we elect corrupt leaders to dominate the political arena. We are responsible if a flood of immorality engulfs our nation and individual families. We are responsible for all this, and will pay a terrible price should we dismiss these truths and fail to act accordingly to save our nation from impending self-imposed slavery!

Finally, Americans must hold fast to their religious and moral beliefs, and they must expose and expel the evil work of those who would undermine the great pillars of morality and freedom! There is no reason that men and women of character, honor, dignity, and truthfulness cannot "step up to the plate" and lead us again into moral sanity!

Therefore, let us call upon such men and women, for the responsibility is entirely up to us!

Chapter Two

"We Lost It"

"Be sober, be vigilant; because your adversary the devil, as a roaring lion, walketh about, seeking whom he may devour." **(1 Peter 5:8)**

"When the righteous are in authority, the people rejoice: but when the wicked beareth rule, the people mourn." **(Proverbs 29:2)**

The responsibility of "We the People," the citizens of America, to ensure that the righteous are in authority has been hampered by the false concept of the "wall of separation" between Church and State.

In 1947 the United States Supreme Court declared that a so-called "wall" must exist between the church and the state in the Everson v. Board of Education decision. Justice Hugo Black took out of context an expression from a letter written by Thomas Jefferson to the Danbury Baptist Association. The Court ignored the true meaning of Jefferson's words, which insisted that a "wall" exist only to forbid the Government from intruding into the affairs of the Church.

Justice Black, however, decided that the reverse was also necessary and that the Church must not be involved with the affairs of the State. There is no mention of the words *church, state,* or *separation* in the First Amendment. That Amendment simply says:

"Congress shall make no law respecting an establishment of religion, or prohibiting the free exercise thereof; or prohibiting the freedom of speech or of the press, or the right of the people peacefully to assemble, and to petition the Government for a redress of grievances."

In other words, Congress could not lawfully establish a national religion, nor prohibit the people from worshipping God, according to their own individual consciences. The "wall" was a "one-way, not two-way wall." The Government was designed to be the servant of the people. The idea of a "wall of separation" would limit the Church and her moral influence over the affairs of the nation and its people.

Another Founding Father, the Reverend John Witherspoon, knew that any nation's strength depended on its spiritual foundation. (Ref. Psalms 11:3) He declared:

"In free states where people have the supreme power in their own hands and must be consulted on all great matters, if there be a general corruption of morals, there can be nothing but confusion. So true is this, that civil liberty cannot long be preserved without virtue...Nothing is more certain than that widespread immorality and corruption of manners make a people ripe for destruction...Beyond a certain point even the best constitution will be ineffectual and slavery must ensue. On the other hand, when the morals of a nation are pure, when true religion and moral principles maintain their vigor, the attempts of the most powerful enemies to oppress them are commonly baffled and disappointed. God grant that in America true religion and civil liberty may be inseparable."

As discussed earlier, America's spiritual state today is evident in the widespread acceptance of moral relativism and situational ethics. The principle of eternal absolute moral truths has been discarded in favor of a "feel-good" pseudo-morality of "live and let live!"

While the American Church slept, the U.S. Supreme Court outlawed the right to pray in the public schools. This occurred in the 1962 court case of Engle v. Vitale. Next, on June 17, 1963, the Supreme Court ruled that

Bible-reading was unconstitutional in the schools, in a lawsuit filed by atheist Madalyn Murray O'Hair. This was followed by an outlawing of the Ten Commandments in the public schools, in 1980 in the court case of Stone v. Graham. In that travesty the Court determined that it was unconstitutional for the Ten Commandments to be posted in a classroom, since the students might be led to read them, meditate upon them, respect them, or obey them. How ridiculous is that!

Was it not James Madison, Chief Architect of the Constitution, who said: *"We have staked the whole future of American civilization not on the power of government. Far from it! We have staked the future of all of our political institutions upon the capacity...of each and all of us to govern ourselves...according to the Ten Commandments of God."*

Even the engravings in the granite and interior of the Federal Buildings in Washington, D.C. bear witness to the same sentiment. The foundations of America were Judeo-Christian, and the Ten Commandments formed the pillars upon which our faith and civil laws rested.

The consequences of removing the influence of God from the public schools has resulted in a decline of SAT scores, rise in violent crime, sexually transmitted diseases, unwed pregnancies, and breakdown of the two-parent family structure. Martin Luther, the Father of the Protestant Reformation, foresaw what would happen if God abandoned the classroom. He declared: *"I am much afraid that schools will prove to be great gates of hell unless they diligently labor in explaining the Holy Scriptures, engraving them in the hearts of youth. I advise no one to place his child where the Scriptures do not reign paramount. Every institution in which men are not increasingly occupied with the Word of God must become corrupt."* **Is there any reason to wonder why we have experienced a rash of school shootings and random violence on various campuses in the recent past?**

The Federal Court has outlawed prayer in school, Bible-reading and the posting of the Ten Commandments, while at the same time, legalizing abortion- on- demand, and homosexual "marriage." Ministers of the Gospel should be fighting for a return to constitutional government. There will not be any room for the preaching of the old-time Gospel if the secularists in the government have their way. How long will Bible-believing preachers be able to preach the straight and narrow message of salvation through Christ alone if the false doctrine of Universalism is the accepted religion? (Universalism is the theological doctrine of salvation, i.e., all religions lead to God.) As it now stands, Universalism is the religion of the United Nations, the European Union, and the emerging North American Union.

Sincere candidates for public office, who claim to be true Christians, will obey his or her oath to preserve, protect, and defend the Constitution of the United States. How then, could a true Christian political candidate make a promise before God and the American people and then turn around and ignore that very promise? These religious hypocrites say they are "Christians," but in reality, only use religious rhetoric to deceive true believers!

The Bible-Believing churches have been deceived by these religious charlatans because the knowledge of God has been erased from American history. According to Benjamin Franklin: "History will afford frequent opportunities of showing the necessity of a public religion from its usefulness to the public; the advantage of a religious character among private persons, the mischiefs of superstition; and the excellency of the Christian religion above all others, ancient or modern."

Benjamin Franklin understood that history, when accurately presented, would demonstrate the need for Christianity because of both the societal and the individual benefits it produces. In fact, the presenting of uncensored, unrevised history actually causes a recognition of the Hand of God! History is God's Providence in human affairs.

Unfortunately, today, American history is presented in such an edited, revised, politically-correct way that God's influence is rarely visible, and the roles of historic godly leaders are unacknowledged.

For example, Americans are taught today that "taxation without representation" was the reason America separated from Great Britain; yet "taxation without representation" was only one reason given in the Declaration of Independence. Numerous grievances condemning judicial activism, religious, and moral issues are never mentioned. In 1792, the King vetoed the charter for America's first missionary society and prevented the printing of an English Bible. Clearly, for many of the Founders, religious freedom issues were an important motivation behind their separation from Great Britain, but that truth is largely ignored today.

As a result of historical revisionism, God is no longer visible in American history. Secular humanists contend that the Founders produced the first intentionally secular government in history. That is a lie because the Declaration of Independence officially acknowledges God in four separate clauses.

As another example, consider the legendary Minutemen. Their leader, the Reverend Jonas Clark, is no longer mentioned, nor the fact that many of the Minutemen were deacons in his church! The Reverend James Caldwell is no longer acknowledged as a key leader of military forces in New Jersey, nor the Reverend John Muhlenberg, who led 300 men from his church against the British.

We no longer know much about the role of ministers and Christian leaders in the founding of our civil government due to historical revisionism. Humanists use revision of our history in an attempt to alter the way people see their heritage in order to cause a change in thinking and public policy.

Consider, if you will, the outcome of these practices. Under the secular view of American history, Americans now believe that the early colonists came to America seeking land and gold rather than for the reason most cited by the colonists, which was religious freedom! Many are now led to believe that the colonies were founded for economic enterprises, even though more than half of the colonies were founded by Gospel ministers for religious purposes, such as evangelization of the Native American Indians. When religion is mentioned at all in most revisionist texts, the emphasis is on the Salem Witch Trials, rather than the Great Awakening Revivals.

There is so much of our God-centered American history that we know little of today. This is especially true concerning our scant knowledge of Black American Religious History. For example, Pastor Lemuel Haynes was involved in several major revolutionary battles and became an ardent admirer of George Washington, regularly preaching sermons on Washington's birthday. This patriot preacher was the first black American to be ordained by the Congregationalists in 1785, pastored a white congregation in Connecticut and awarded an honorary degree in 1804. Yet, who today has ever heard of Pastor Lemuel Haynes? Then there is Reverend John Marrant, the first black American minister to evangelize among the American Indians. The Reverend Richard Allen, who gained his freedom from slavery, served in the American Revolution, and founded America's first black Methodist denomination.

Who today knows the story of the Reverend Hiram Rhodes Revels, the black American missionary, who became the first black U.S. Senator?

How about the Reverend Henry Garnet, the first black American to deliver a sermon in Congress? Who has learned today that nearly every southern Republican Party was started by black Americans, who were all Republicans and many were also ministers?

I truly believe we have lost our truthful and complete telling of American religious history and a revival of such is long overdue! History is God's providence in human affairs, and it is time for Americans onsce again to become aware of the remarkable Hand of God throughout our history. This is why the framers of the Constitution spoke about the fact that only a free and moral people, in other words, a nation of godly people with common spiritual and social values, were capable of self-government.

Chapter Three

"It's Time to Get It Back"

Moral and Political Quotes to Ponder:

"Politics ought to be the part-time profession of every citizen who would protect the rights and privileges of free people and who would preserve what is good and fruitful in our national heritage." –Dwight D. Eisenhower.

"A government which robs Peter to pay Paul can always depend on the support of Paul" –George Bernard Shaw.

"Vote for the man who promises least; he'll be the least disappointing." –Bernard Baruch.

"Giving money and power to government is like giving whiskey and car keys to teenage boys." –P. J. O'Rourke

"The inherent vice of capitalism is the unequal sharing of the blessings. The inherent blessings of socialism is the equal sharing of the misery." –Winston Churchill

"Deeper thinkers who look everywhere for the mysterious causes of poverty, ignorance, crime and war need look no further than their own mirrors. We are all born into this world poor and ignorant, and with thoroughly selfish and barbaric impulses. Those of us who turn out any other way, do so largely through the efforts of others, who civilized us before we got big enough to do too much damage to the world or ourselves." —*Thomas Sowell*

"The price good men pay for indifference to public affairs is to be ruled by evil men." —*Plato*

"Of two evils choose neither." —*Charles Haddon Spurgeon*

"Never turn your back on a threatened danger and try to run away from it. If you do that, you will double the danger. But if you meet it promptly and without flinching, you will reduce the danger by half. Never run away from anything, never." —*Winston Churchill*

"We hold these Truths to be self-evident, that all Men are created equal, that they are endowed by their Creator with certain unalienable Rights, that among these are Life, Liberty, and the Pursuit of Happiness. That to secure these Rights, Governments are instituted among Men, deriving their just Powers from the Consent of the Governed. That whenever any Form of Government becomes destructive of these Ends, it is the Right of the People to alter or to abolish it, and to institute new Government, laying its Foundation on such Principles, and organizing its Powers in such Forms, as to them shall seem most likely to effect their Safety and Happiness." —*The Declaration of Independence.*

According to the Declaration, we are in need of a non-violent political revolution in order to return our government to its constitutional boundaries. "We the People" must "step up to the political plate" and rid our government of the "cancer of party politics!"

Party politics, working through the two-party system, has allowed the Legislative, Executive, and Judicial system to serve special interests groups instead of the American people. The electorate has been deceived into fighting each other, using divisions such as Republican/Democrat/Right-Wing/Left-Wing/Conservative/Liberal, etc. Meanwhile, the U.S. House of Representatives, U.S. Senate, the President, and the Supreme Court have a blank check to rob ordinary American citizens blind!

By framing the battle and the debate in terms of which political party controls the government in Washington, D.C, the elitists were able to control the entire nation and virtually eliminating the government "of, by, and for the people!"

Thank God, this deception is finally being discovered because individual groups of concerned citizens in America have discovered the key for returning all political power in America back to the people! The fact that people are finally waking up to the corruption in government and crying out for change is proof that this is truly an idea from God whose time has come! No satanic force on earth can stop an idea whose time has come!

The vision is to disregard all considerations of political party affiliations, issues, agendas, candidates, etc., and as the Declaration states, "abolish or alter" it and institute new government! We need term limits on all branches of government! All we as American citizens, who are eligible to vote, have to do is to fire all incumbents who have violated their oath of office to uphold the Constitution of the United States. Simply replace them with sound Constitutional candidates, who will uphold the Constitution, and then "hold their feet to the fire" as well.

Question: "Is this idea insane?" The answer is No. Insanity is doing the same thing over and over and expecting different results. Firing the rascals in government will be just the opposite of insanity. In fact, it will restore political and spiritual sanity to the American people!

The political insanity in Washington is not Republicans, Democrats, Conservatives, Liberals, Issues, or Ideologies, that keep the average American citizen constantly at each other's throat. Remember the idea of "divide and conquer?" No, the insanity is made up of the political elite, who tell us that there are issues that should divide us and we should continue fighting each other for the "soul of America!" The true "soul of America" however, is this: *"We the People of the United States are supposed to have all of the political power and we are supposed to be free, according to the United States Constitution!"*

Another Question: Are you a Conservative who hates the tyranny of a socialist state? Well, we are all being enslaved by the elite in Washington, D.C. Are you a Liberal who hates war? Well, we are all at war with each other, while they simply laugh in our faces! In other words, we need to "clean house" in Washington, D.C. and start fresh. Incumbency is problematic because fallen human beings get too comfortable when they get too much power. Remember the old saying: "Power corrupts, and absolute Power corrupts absolutely"! We need "new wine, in new wineskins" in Washington, D.C., and then hold them accountable to be true part-time servants of "We the People" who elect and send them there to represent us! Too simplistic, you say? Could it be that the problem is the American people themselves? We need term limits, or part-time elected officials. Perhaps we have forgotten the proper constitutional role of members of Congress. We have forgotten that they work for us, that is the reason we elect them in the first place. We have forgotten that they are bound, by oath, to uphold the U.S. Constitution, and this Constitution strictly limits their lust for political and economic power. Wouldn't it be a great blessing if our children and grandchildren inherit a country served by true patriots who voluntarily obey the U.S. Constitution? We can make a difference and take our beloved country back, by simply refusing to re-elect those scoundrels who have been using incumbency to play us for the fool!

Never mind the elites who control the media. They will tell you about all the terrible things "the other party" is doing, or has done, while making you believe that "the other party" controls the media in some fashion. The truth of the matter is this: those who control the media control both major political parties! Never mind those who object to firing these incumbents because of political pork they have provided to their district. Never mind the objection that says firing the incumbent will only help "the other party" advance their own agenda. We must understand "business as usual" will never stop in Washington, D.C. if we keep on "voting as usual!" Doesn't that make sense? It certainly does to me and many others, who are sick and tired of being sick and tired! We must obey the Constitution and the Declaration of Independence tells us to "send them packing!"

"We the People" are the key to this nation's healing. "We the People" can perform "political surgery" in Washington, D.C. by sending the corrupt politicians home! We have the power to vote the rascals out, and vote constitutionalists in! If we neglect this responsibility much longer, the day will surely come when we will no longer have the right to vote for constitutional government! That is political slavery!

The issue today is the same as it has been throughout all of American History. Shall we be allowed to govern ourselves, or shall we be ruled by a small socialist elite? If we govern ourselves and reject the current madness in Washington, here are some of the benefits we will see:

1. By firing them, we will remind them that "We the People" are the boss. The elites have forgotten why they were elected in the first place. They were sent to Washington to serve us, not the other way around.

2. We will let both political parties know that the "party is over" and the Government is being rescued by the people, according to the Constitution.

3. We will also let the newly-elected officials know that they too will be fired if they violate their oath to obey the Constitution.

4. We will eliminate special interest groups and lobbyists, who legally bribe elected officials to get political favors at taxpayers' expense.

5. We will send a stern message to those elected officials who have political ambition to gain power by reminding them of term limits which will be imposed.

6. We will let the Executive Branch know that the President won't have a rubber- stamp Congress to pass whatever law he proposes. He will also know that Congress is the predominate branch of government under the Constitution, followed by the Executive, and then the Judicial Branch.

As I said before, this is a vision and idea whose time has come. It is also constitutional! I want to live in a country where I can be proud of my elected officials because they are true patriots upholding and obeying the Constitution.

We must mobilize ourselves to change the character of the House and Senate. We must stop focusing on the Presidency and start focusing on Congress. That is where "We the People" can make a real difference! It will take courage and hard work, and it will be revolutionary in every sense of the word. It will take a united effort of "We the People" of the United States of America. It will take a national uprising. It can and must be done! It's time to take our country back!

Conclusion

By the end of the 1950's, Americans were beginning to witness a breakdown in their political institutions as meaningful forces for good. Most politicians were convinced that the solution to social problems was federal-funded programs. They believed that any problem could be solved by simply spending enough of the taxpayers' money. This false idea soon bloated the Federal Government with social "pork-barrel" spending, and increased the federal budget deficit. These programs made many people dependent upon government support, which became a form of economic slavery. It gave birth to a sense of false entitlement, hopelessness, apathy, and despair. This, in turn, bred contempt for authority and an increase in lawlessness. The root of the problem, as we have stated, was the steady decline in emphasis on Biblical morality, ethics, and the principles of the U.S. Constitution.

How did the American Church respond to these things? We in the Church became self-righteous, arrogant, and sanctimonious, instead of humbling ourselves through fasting and repentance in order to seek God's Divine favor.

In the Book of Ezra, the scribe, we see that he humbly and faithfully led the way to national repentance in Israel. He fasted and humbled himself before God in sincerity, thereby setting an example so powerful that it brought spiritual conviction to the hearts and minds of his fellow countrymen. As a result, a move of repentance toward God, swept through the Jewish population. This is what's needed in America today--a true spiritual and moral revival of repentance among God's people. This allows God to truly change the hearts, minds, and lives of the people who submit to His correction and discipline.

A true spiritual awakening in America must begin according to the scripture:

"If My people who are called by My name will humble themselves, and pray and seek My face, and turn from their wicked ways, then I will hear from heaven, and will forgive their sin and heal their land." (2 Chronicles 7:14)

After the terrorist attack on September 11, 2001, spiritual leaders all over America were quoting 2 Chronicles 7:14 and leading people in prayer. However, it was very short-lived, and soon it was "business as usual." God requires true humility, brokenness, and repentance, by inviting the Lord to search our hearts and expose the things that displease Him. This, in turn, leads to true changes in the hearts and lives of people that bring them closer to God. Then God begins to restore and heal the land during times of trouble.

During the birth of this nation, it was the Continental Congress that unified the prayers of the people. It set July 20, 1775 as a day of humiliation and prayer for the restoration of the just civil and religious privileges of America, which was observed throughout the colonies. Thomas Jefferson wrote that this action helped lift the spirits of Americans, and caused them to focus more clearly on what was really important. This is needed in America today on a collective and massive scale!

I believe healing will come about in our government when a true revival happens among God's people in the Church. While political activism, as I mentioned in the last chapter, is needed, it will not be sustained without the work of the Holy Spirit working through Christ's Church. We have been fighting against Government corruption for decades without lasting success, because of the lack of spiritual renewal.

The Scriptures declare:

"And I sought for a man among them, that should make up the hedge, and stand in the gap before me for the land, that I should not destroy it: but I found none. Therefore have I poured out mine indignation upon them, I have consumed them with the fire of my wrath: their own way have I recompensed upon their heads, saith the Lord God." (Ezekiel 22: 30–31)

We Christians in America have lost many of our religious liberties, and the right to free exercise of our faith, despite the fact that these things are explicitly protected by the U.S. Constitution through the First Amendment. This chastening and loss of religious freedom is meant to humble us and bring us back to our "spiritual senses"! We must remember the "Battle is not ours, but God's." (2 Chronicles 20:15) The Church in America is called to "stand in the gap" for our nation before it is too late. True sacrificial devotion to God and His purposes is what the Lord requires from His people in the churches of America today.

In conclusion, only when we become willing to respond to each other with the kind of love that covers the "gaps" in our lives can we expect God to use us to bring healing to our beloved land. We need the Agape love, which releases God's anointing, when there is "*unity in the Spirit in the bond of peace.*"(Ephesians 4:3) This will strengthen the Body of Christ, which is His Church, and preserve this once great nation of ours!

God will bless America when we recognize that He alone is the only answer to restoring Morality and Freedom. Therefore, let us who are politically-active Christians, replace immoral and unprincipled leaders with those who will be accountable to God. Then, we will see a "Dynamic Duo" of Morality and Freedom in America once again!

Printed in the United States
By Bookmasters